...TO DO TO FIND
LOVE IN THE
MODERN WORLD

CLEOPATRA VALENTINE

Published in the UK in 2019 by Short Books
Unit 316, ScreenWorks,
22 Highbury Grove, London N5 2ER

10 9 8 7 6 5 4 3 2 1

A CIP catalogue record for this book is available
from the British Library.

ISBN 978-1-78072-408-9

Printed and bound in Great Britain by
CPI Group (UK) Ltd, Croydon, CR0 4YY

Page Layouts by Short Books
Cover design by Two Associates

Introduction

In a world of connectivity, portable tech and ever growing populations, it should be easier than ever to find love – and yet so often it isn't. Is the modern world conspiring to keep us apart, rather than bring us together?

Never fear! Romance may be an art form, but it's one that you can curate. And the imaginative activities, tips and ideas compiled here are designed to help you do just that.

Whether you are new to the dating game, an old hand running out of tricks, or just completely frazzled by the whole escapade, this book is the booster shot your love life needs.

1.

Brew up a 'Divine Love' tea.

½ cinnamon stick   ½ orange peel
1 star anise   ½ tsp ginger
½ tsp coriander seeds ½ vanilla bean

Brew these aphrodisiac ingredients in boiling water
for 2-3 minutes and strain into a mug. And voilà!

2.

Liven up your image:
Go to a zoo and pose with
a lion or a tiger for your
Tinder profile.

3.

Categorise your past lovers by which sort of novel they would most likely appear in:

1. Any Mills & Boon novel

2. *Pride and Prejudice*

3. Jilly Cooper's *Riders*

4. *The Notebook*

5. *Fifty Shades of Grey*

6. *The Picture of Dorian Gray*

7. Stephen King's *Misery*

8. Stephen King's *It*

4.

Strike up a conversation with someone on public transport.

Icebreaker
Street

5.

List the three most attractive things about yourself.

_____

_____

_____

6.

Host a dinner party and ask each of your friends to invite a single guest.

7.

Get inspired by going to see a rom-com.

PRODUCTION
"GENERIC ROM-COM"

DIRECTOR
AMANDA HUGGENKISS

SCENE 6 | TAKE 1

Take notes!

8.

Play 'Snog, Marry, Avoid'.

9.

Change your perspective.

Get the global take on love by checking out these proverbs from around the world. ➡

"Love itself is calm; turbulence arrives from individuals."

Chinese

"Love sickness hurts but does not kill."

Mexican

"In love beggar and king are equal."

Indian

"Love has to be shown by deeds, not words."

Swahili

"A day lasts until it's chased away but love lasts until the grave."

Irish

"Try to reason about love and you will lose your reason."

French

"The heart that loves is always young."

Greek

10.

Seen someone reading a book you've heard lots about?

Great!

Strike up a conversation about it.

(You don't have to have read it, you just need to know enough about the author, the story or the themes to ask a few good questions.)

11.

Love is a truly statistical thing.

Robin carried out a survey on 100 women in his local area to find out what hobbies they might have in common with him. The results are shown below.

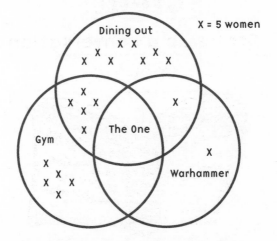

Q1. What are the chances that a fellow gym-goer would consider Robin's offer of a meal out?

Q2. Statistically, nobody ticks all the boxes. Which hobby should Robin sacrifice in his search for love?

Q3. How many potential partners might he meet at the local Warhammer fanclub dinner?

12.

Identify on the scales below what sort of personality you are looking for in a partner.

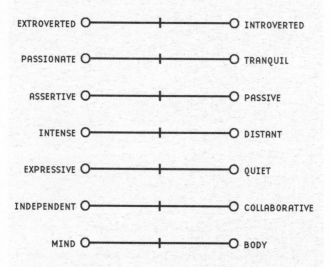

EXTROVERTED	O———┼———O	INTROVERTED
PASSIONATE	O———┼———O	TRANQUIL
ASSERTIVE	O———┼———O	PASSIVE
INTENSE	O———┼———O	DISTANT
EXPRESSIVE	O———┼———O	QUIET
INDEPENDENT	O———┼———O	COLLABORATIVE
MIND	O———┼———O	BODY

But always be open-minded to adjusting these expectations...

13.

Now on these scales try to plot the personality of your previous partner.

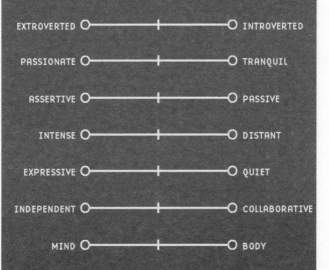

EXTROVERTED	O————┼————O	INTROVERTED
PASSIONATE	O————┼————O	TRANQUIL
ASSERTIVE	O————┼————O	PASSIVE
INTENSE	O————┼————O	DISTANT
EXPRESSIVE	O————┼————O	QUIET
INDEPENDENT	O————┼————O	COLLABORATIVE
MIND	O————┼————O	BODY

Be careful not to make the same mistakes again...

14.

Comb your hair
and moisturise.

15.

Here is a handy guide to avoiding profile pic faux pas:

Don't use an image that's more than 12 months old

Don't use too many insta filters

Don't have multiple people in the image

Don't use a photo of a model or celebrity

Don't use a bathroom mirror selfie

Don't wear too few items of clothing

16.

Move on from your old relationships by categorising your exes on the pie chart opposite.

a. egotistical   b. didn't do chores
c. snorer   d. nice, no edge
e. unreliable   f. bad dancer

17.

Treat all of life's inconveniences
(long queues, traffic jams, delayed
flights) as chances for romance.

TIME	DESTINATION	STATUS
14.05	Budapest	DELAYED
14.05	Tokyo	DELAYED
14.10	Rome	DELAYED
14.15	Paris	DELAYED
14.15	New York	DELAYED
14.25	Helsinki	DELAYED
14.25	Manchester	DELAYED
14.30	Love	ON TIME
14.35	Sydney	DELAYED
14.40	Prague	DELAYED
14.40	Los Angeles	DELAYED
14.45	Mexico City	DELAYED
14.50	Guernsey	DELAYED
14.50	Glasgow	DELAYED
14.55	Barcelona	DELAYED

18.

Write a list of your five favourite books.

They'll make good conversation topics.

1 ....

2 ....

3 ....

4 ....

5 ....

♫ 19. ♪♫

Learn to play "You Are My Sunshine" on guitar.

E   **E**
You are my sunshine, my only sunshine,

A   **E**
You make me happy when skies are grey.

A   **E**
You'll never know, dear, how much I love you.

B7 E
Please don't take my sunshine away.

20.

Join a ballroom dancing class.

While *Strictly* hasn't made us all better dancers, it has taught us that dancing leads inexorably to romance...

 **21.**

Verbal reasoning quiz.

Get used to the love lingo
by picking the odd one out
in each of these lists:

1. Kind, Caring, Considerate, Keeper

Odd one out: _____

2. Blush, Swoon, Spurn, Simper

Odd one out: _____

~~~~~~

3. Hug, Tickle, Spoon, Cutch

Odd one out: _____

4. Pretty, Handsome, Vain, Beautiful

Odd one out: _____

5. To date, To ghost, To dump, To blank

Odd one out: _____

~~~~~~

Answers: 1. Keeper, 2.Spurn, 3. Tickle,
4. Vain, 5. To Date

22.

Pick a passion.

Whether it's alternative music, psychology, far-eastern culture or the history of the great American novel - find something you enjoy and learn everything you can about it.

Your **enthusiasm** will create a **positive atmosphere** during conversions.

23.

Try this spell to discover your true love:

In the morning peel a lemon and place two equal size pieces of the peel together in your pocket.

Leave them there all day.

Before bed take the peels out of your pocket and rub the legs of the bed with them, then place them under your pillow.

The person you dream of, you will surely marry.

24.

Do the age-old rules of love still apply?
Watch these modern adaptations of
Pride and Prejudice and see for yourself.

- [ ] *Pride and Prejudice* with Colin Firth
- [ ] *Bridget Jones's Diary*
- [ ] *Bride and Prejudice*
- [ ] *Pride and Prejudice* with Keira Knightley
- [ ] *Before the Fall*
- [ ] *Death Comes to Pemberley*
- [ ] *The Lizzie Bennet Diaries*
- [ ] *Pride and Prejudice and Zombies*

25.

Memorise this sonnet to impress your love interest:

Bright star, would I were stedfast as thou art—
    Not in lone splendour hung aloft the night
    And watching, with eternal lids apart,
        Like nature's patient, sleepless Eremite,
The moving waters at their priestlike task
    Of pure ablution round earth's human shores,
    Or gazing on the new soft-fallen mask
    Of snow upon the mountains and the moors—
No—yet still stedfast, still unchangeable,
    Pillow'd upon my fair love's ripening breast,
    To feel for ever its soft fall and swell,
        Awake for ever in a sweet unrest,
Still, still to hear her tender-taken breath,
And so live ever—or else swoon to death.

John Keats

26.

Book yourself in for ten weeks of therapy now to save the hassle later.

"I really thought I was in love, but it turned out it was just acid reflux..."

27. Design a lover's tattoo featuring the name of your crush and optimistically get it tattooed on your body.

28.

Topics not to be discussed on a first date:

❌ Donald Trump
(hereinafter referred to as
"He who shall remain nameless")

❌ Your many allergies

❌ Car insurance
(unless it is their job)

❌ Your ex

❌ That time you were arrested
for stalking your ex

❌ Movies starring Tom Cruise
(come on, you're better than that)

29.

Practise that famed piece of
facial acrobatics, guaranteed
to ignite a lover's interest...

Raising one eyebrow.

30.

Imagine all the things you could buy if you were in a couple with someone.

- A double bed?
- An M&S Dine In Meal Deal for 2?
- A tandem bike?
- A Travel Together railcard?
- A see-saw?

The possibilities are endless...

31.
Dance!

Even if you don't know how.*

Especially if you don't know how.

32.

Borrow a small dog and take it everywhere you go to show you are a caring, responsible member of society.

Yes, I am cute. And a guaranteed conversation starter.

33.

Can you work out these romantic anagrams?

DIVETOON

MOCTRAIN

SENTRESEND

GINSIKS

RAGEMAIR

34.

Write a letter to your future partner.

Think about what you want from a relationship, what you can offer, what you hope they will help you become and what you will be like together.

To my future partner,

....

....

....

....

....

....

....

....

....

....

....

35.

Phone a

friend.

Put your trust in those who know you best and ask your friends to set you up.

36.

Establish a good pre-date routine.

- Put on some good music.
- Make any necessary reservations.
- Iron the outfit you'll wear.
- Pick up some flowers or a small gift.
- Brush your teeth and go to the loo.

Give yourself plenty of time to carry out the routine before every date — it will set you in the right frame of mind.

37.

Rediscover your confidence by writing three affirmations about what makes you a good lover:

#1 ....

#2 ....

#3 ....

Make sure they are (i) present tense, (ii) positive and (iii) specific.

38.

Love can blossom from unlikely beginnings. Check out these first words uttered between lovers:

"Did you expect a present? Are you fond of presents?"
Mr Rochester to Jane Eyre

"If it be love indeed, tell me how much."
Cleopatra to Mark Antony

"If I profane with my unworthiest hand This holy shrine, the gentle fine is this..."
Romeo to Juliet

"She is tolerable, but not handsome enough to tempt me."
Mr Darcy to Elizabeth (overheard)

"Has anyone seen a toad? Neville's lost one."
Hermione to Ron

39.

Draw up your online profile
using these prompts:

My dream dinner guest from
history would be:

The signature dish I would
cook for them is:

The most spontaneous thing
I've ever done is:

My ideal Sunday afternoon
would involve:

The title for my autobiography
would be:

40.

Write the opening scene
for the rom-com movie
adaptation of your life.

And once the scene is set, go
out and put events in motion!

41.

Relationships can be difficult.

But probably not as difficult as a sudoku where the numbers have been changed into symbols...

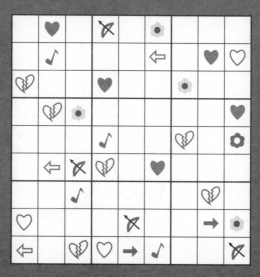

42.

Download a marriage counselling podcast to reassure yourself that you aren't missing anything!

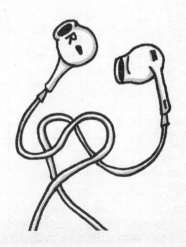

43.

Arrange the ultimate "blind date":

go dining

in the

dark

44.

Try out these guaranteed conversation starters to fill any awkward silences:

- Are you a cat or a dog person? Or neither of the above?

- What's the absolute first thing you would buy if you won a million pounds?

- Do you come here often? You clearly like the food.

- Would you rather have bananas for fingers or sneeze every time you smiled?

- Soooo... have you seen any good movies lately?

45.

Write a love poem.

(But, for goodness sake, don't
show it to anyone.)

46.

Learn how to read the signs.

You can tell somebody is interested in you romantically by looking out for these non-verbal cues...

- ♥ Looking at you, looking away and then looking back.
- ♥ Feet pointing in your direction.
- ♥ Making adjustments to their appearance.
- ♥ Playing with their hair.
- ♥ Displaying an open wrist or palm.
- ♥ Holding an open body posture (arms away from the body).
- ♥ Leaning towards you.
- ♥ Mirroring your actions.

47.

Whip up this easy beetroot dip.

Beetroot has been a known aphrodisiac since Roman times due to its high levels of boron, a mineral involved in the production of sex hormones.

250g creme fraîche
¼ a cucumber, grated
1 cooked beetroot, grated
juice of ¼ lemon

5 mint leaves
sprig of dill, chopped
½ teaspoon olive oil
pinch of salt

Mix all the ingredients togther in a bowl and enjoy with the lucky guy or gal in your life!

48.

Go to a karaoke singles night

And siiiing your way into someone's heart!

49.

Devise your own dinner date menu.

Starter

♥ ♥ ♥

....

....

....

Main

♥ ♥ ♥

....

....

....

Dessert

♥ ♥ ♥

....

....

....

50. Can you identify these romantic flowers?

1.

Has five flat-faced, cobalt-blue petals;
also known as scorpion grass.

2.

Boasts a cluster of petals and a
pleasant scent; beware of prickles.

3.

Features five white petals with
long stamens; has a lemony smell.

4.

Has richly coloured, heart-shaped petals
with one broad petal poiting downwards.

51.

Make sure you get your beauty sleep.

Here are some tips:

- 💤 Don't drink caffeine after 3pm
- 💤 Take a hot bath before bed
- 💤 Exercise in the late afternoon
- 💤 Use an eye mask and/or ear plugs
- 💤 Ban screens from the bedroom
- 💤 Practise progressive muscle relaxation

52.

GET LOST!

And ask for directions.

Use every wrong turn as a chance for flirtation.

53.

Try out some
of these

cheesy
chat-up lines.

WARNING:
USE AT YOUR OWN RISK

Can I follow you home..?
My parents always told me to follow my dreams.

Your hand looks heavy...
Let me hold it for you.

Are you a magician..?
Because whenever I look at you, everyone else disappears!

I seem to have lost my phone number...
Can I have yours?

I'm not a photographer...
But I can picture you and me together.

54.

What's past is past.

On the page opposite, write out what happened on your most disastrous date ever.

Then tear out the page and burn it.

55.

Compile your own love playlist.

A beautiful song triggers the release of dopamine — the passion hormone.

1 ....

....

2 ....

....

3 ....

....

4 ....

....

5 ....

....

56.

Here's how to tell if someone likes you by their star sign:

ARIES
Will be forward and outgoing; you'll know.

TAURUS
May take their time, but will be generous with gifts.

GEMINI
Will be flirty and persistent.

CANCER
Will be protective and offer home comforts — they may cook for you.

LEO
Will simply want to spend time with you.

VIRGO
May be guarded, but will help you with tasks.

LIBRA
Will be charismatic with everyone, but desperate to please just you.

SCORPIO
You'll have to catch them off guard for signs of interest — will be quiet but intense.

SAGITTARIUS
Will want you to join them on their next adventure.

CAPRICORN
Will tell you, but you'll have to earn it.

AQUARIUS
Will want you with them on their personal crusades.

PISCES
Will be quiet with you at first, but will really open up if you give them the chance.

57.

Here are some useful phrases for when you are on a date with an outdoorsy thrill-seeker.

▲ What's the weirdest place you've ever set up camp?

▲ I would probably take the challenge of swimming the Channel, but not swimming the Thames.

▲ I think Bear Grylls deliberately got stung by the jellyfish to create a new urine-related survival scenario.

▲ Is base jumping or white-water rafting more dangerous?

▲ I wouldn't say I've *done* a bungee jump, but I have watched someone do one on TV.

58.

Make psychoanalysis do the work:

What do you see
in the inkblot?

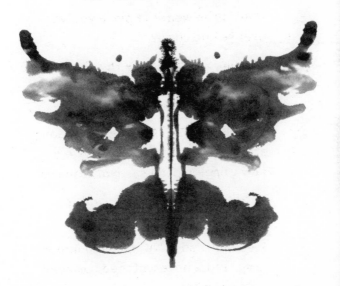

Ask every potential partner, and if they see
the same thing as you, start making plans.

59.
Going Dutch?
Use the table opposite to help work out the bill.

	Me	My date	TOTAL
Starter			
Main			
Dessert			
Sides			
Water			
Wine			
Beer			
SUB-TOT			
Tip			
TOTAL			

60.

Match up the famous quotes about love opposite with the movies below.

1. *It's a Wonderful Life*

2. *Knocked Up*

3. *Back to the Future*

4. *Bridget Jones's Diary*

5. *Notting Hill*

6. *Gone With the Wind*

Answers: 1e, 2c, 3f, 4a, 5d, 6b

a) "I like you very much. Just as you are."

b) "You should be kissed, and often, and by someone who knows how."

c) "Marriage is like a tense, unfunny version of *Everybody Loves Raymond*, only it doesn't last 22 minutes."

d) "After all, I'm just a girl, standing in front of a boy, asking him to love her."

e) "You want the moon? Just say the word, and I'll throw a lasso around it and pull it down."

f) "I'm your density. I mean, your destiny."

61.

Call your parents and ask them how they first met.

Be sure to tell the story on each and every first date.

Twice.

62.

Message your teenage crush.

Better a "whoops" than a "what if?"

63.

A healthy relationship is about give and take, so be clear about what you want.

Use these tips for how to **communicate assertively.**

Remember: This isn't about being argumentative or confrontational, but rather about prompting open conversation.

Say how you are feeling:

"I am concerned..."

Say what it's about:

"...that you don't want to tell your friends about us..."

Say what you would like to happen:

"...so I'd really like you to introduce me to them this weekend..."

Ask for confirmation:

"Can we do that please?"

And, if they don't agree:

"Why not?"

64.

Pick your ideal romantic honeymoon destination.

65.

Speak the language of love.

Learn these essential romantic Italian phrases:

> ### Tu sei l'unico per me
>
> (You're the only one for me)

> ### Sono dipendente dei tuoi baci
>
> (I'm addicted to your kisses)

> ### Tu sei il sole del mio giorno
>
> (You are the sunshine of my day)

66.

Here are some useful phrases for when you are on a date with a vegan.

- Apparently, one vegan spares the lives of approximately 30 animals every year.

- Veganism is not just about food, right? What lifestyle changes should I be making?

- Did you know that soy milk has nearly as much protein as cow's milk?

- The *Cowspiracy* documentary on Netflix totally changed my outlook on food.

- You know what they say, "You can't make guacamole without smashing avocados."

67.

Clean your bedroom.

68.

Loiter in an art gallery and strike up a conversation about a painting.

The thing I love about Picasso is that he's so... *courageous.*

69.

Fancy a spoon?

Follow the Welsh tradition and carve a spoon for your love.

100% satisfaction guaranteed *

* Terms and conditions apply

70.

Love hurts.

Take inspiration from these famous musicians and turn your past relationships into hit album titles:

For Emma, Forever Ago _____ Bon Iver

Here, My Dear _____ Marvin Gaye

Back to Black _____ Amy Winehouse

Blood on the Tracks _____ Bob Dylan

Rumours _____ Fleetwood Mac

It's Not Me, It's You _____ Lilly Allen

71.

Looking for your knight in shining armour?

Try accidentally stumbling in front of an attractive stranger and see if they come to your aid.

72.

Use these classy one-liners to show off your Good Sense Of Humour

What do you call sad coffee?

A despresso.

Why did Tony go out with a prune?

Because he couldn't find a date!

How do you drown a hipster?

In the mainstream.

What do squirrels give their dates on Valentine's Day?

Forget-me-nuts.

73.

Want to be truer to your personal style?

Write down your own top one-liners:

Set up:

_____

Punchline:

_____

Set up:

_____

Punchline:

_____

74.

Multiple choice.

Decide the best course of action in each of these situations.

1. The person you like hasn't replied to your message today. Do you:

   a) Message them every few minutes until they respond.
   b) Delete their number from your contacts.
   c) Play it cool and wait a little longer; if they don't reply it's their loss.

2. It's becoming clear you have been stood up by your date. Do you:

   a) Track their location via GPS and seek them out.
   b) Move on; strike up a casual conversation with someone else.
   c) Strike up a conversation with someone else, but send a selfie to your date.

3. You think you've found someone you really like. Do you:

a) Test the water by casually dropping hints with a mutual friend.
b) Write them a letter expressing the depth of your emotions.
c) Give them the silent treatment - they'll cotton on eventually.

4. You just met your new partner's friends. You fancy one of them. Do you:

a) Decide you've made your choice and stick with it regardless.
b) Lay the groundwork for a polyamorous relationship.
c) Respectfully break the relationship and see how you feel in a few weeks' time.

5. You may have just experienced love at first sight. Do you:

a) Follow that person and study their daily routine.
b) Ask them out for a coffee - be confident but not overbearing.
c) Give them a cheeky wink and offer them your business card.

75.

When in doubt...

Swipe right.

76.
Exercise with your love interest.

Exercise produces the same
physiological effects as sexual
attraction — and body and mind
can easily conflate the two.

77.

Keypad conundrums.

Reveal these encoded truisms about love.

Each letter has been replaced by its corresponding number on a mobile phone keypad.

Example:

B	E	A	U	T	Y		I	S		O	N	L	Y
2	3	2	8	8	9		4	7		6	6	5	9

S	K	I	N		D	E	E	P
7	5	4	6		3	3	3	7

2
ABC

— — — — —   — — — —   — — —
6 6 6 3 9   2 2 6 8   2 8 9

— —   — — — —
6 3   5 6 8 3

3
DEF

— — —   — —   — — — —   — —
2 5 5   4 7   3 2 4 7   4 6

— — — —   — — —   — — —
5 6 8 3   2 6 3   9 2 7

4
GHI

— — — —   — —   — — —
5 6 8 3   4 7   2 5 5

— — — — — —
2 7 6 8 6 3

Answers overleaf

Keypad conundrums.

Solutions:

1. Love is blind

2. Money can't buy me love

3. All is fair in love and war

4. Love is all around

78.

Remember these restaurant rules.

- Never order the noodle-based dish.

- Look up the menu beforehand (you'll appear more decisive when you make your choice).

- Be kind to waiting staff — and tip well (within reason).

- Have a friend prepped to call with a fake "emergency" if you need to make an escape.

79.

You can never be too keen.
Write a list of your favourite
children's names.

Girls	Boys
....	....
....	....
....	....
....	....
....	....
....	....
....	....

80.

Practise this empowering yoga pose.

Warrior II

- An excellent pose for achieving clarity.
- Helps you dismiss frustrations of the past.
- A stance that brings with it feelings of self confidence and reassurance.

81.

Identify precisely what is going on in that brain of yours.

Testosterone and Oestrogen

The key sex hormones behind the first, physical attraction.

Opioid receptors

Once these are triggered by the sight or smell of a love interest, endorphins and hormones are released.

Cortisol

Levels of this stress hormone rise with the feeling of new love.

Adrenaline and Noradrenaline

The neurotransmitters that speed up the heartbeat in a "fight or flight" response.

Oxytocin

This is the attachment molecule, which floods the system during a hug (or more).

82.

Be prepared to do the washing up.

83.

Not sure if it's really love?
Get your head around this
tongue twister, and you'll
know the answer:

Love's a feeling you feel
when you feel you're going
to feel the feeling you've
never felt before.

Got it? Good.

84.

There's no term for them in English, but now you can name them, perhaps they'll help guide you in your search for The One.

Koi no yokan

ORIGIN: Japan

LITERAL TRANSLATION: The premonition of love

MEANING: This is knowing, upon first meeting someone, that you are destined to be with them.

Chi ama me, ama il mio cane

<u>ORIGIN</u>: Italy

<u>LITERAL TRANSLATION</u>: He who loves me loves my dog

<u>MEANING</u>: In other words, if someone loves you, they love you for who you are.

Tu eres mi media naranja

<u>ORIGIN</u>: Spain

<u>LITERAL TRANSLATION</u>: You are my half orange

<u>MEANING</u>: Assuming you were always destined to be a whole orange, this person is your soulmate. You might say they complete you.

La douleur exquise

<u>ORIGIN</u>: France

<u>LITERAL TRANSLATION</u>: The exquisite pain

<u>MEANING</u>: In fact, a very specific, romantic pain — the heartbreaking pain of wanting someone you can't have.

85.

Here are some useful phrases for when you are on a date with someone who is mad about sci-fi.

- There's no question about it, Greedo did *not* shoot first.

- I never understood how Captain Picard's Borg assimilation process could be fully reversed.

- Deckard would certainly pass the Turing Test, but I'm not sure about the Voight-Kampff Test.

- *Dark City* was a much better film than *The Matrix*.

- You can have multi-million dollar CGI at your disposal, but nothing beats the time-lapse photography in *The Time Machine*.

86.

Pick a dating activity that requires physical proximity.

How about asking for help
with that golf swing?

87.

Always always always:

Listen well.

88.

Work out which of these facts are true and which are false.

1. The world record for the longest marriage is 86 years.

2. The country with the highest divorce rate is Belarus.

3. When two lovers gaze into each other's eyes, their heart rates synchronise.

4. The longest underwater kiss lasted for more than 3 minutes.

5. Half of all marriages end in divorce.

Answers overleaf

#88 Love facts:
Answers.

1. **TRUE:** The marriage of Herbert and Zelmyra Fisher in the US.

2. **FALSE:** It is actually the Maldives. Belarus is second.

3. **TRUE:** They also have similar rates of respiration.

4. **TRUE:** 3 min 24 sec to be precise.

5. **FALSE:** And, indeed, in the UK and the US, divorce rates are falling.

89.

Write a horoscope reading and give it to your love interest.

(Fill it with positive suggestions but keep the details suitably vague.)

....
....
....
....
....
....
....
....
....
....
....
....

90.

Find out your crush's favourite song and hum it gently when you are near them.

It will help them realise that you are, indeed, **The One**

91.

Train your brain

so you're ready to deploy some witty wordplay next time the need arises.

Try this exercise:

How many words can you make from the letters in:

BE MY
VALENTINE

92.
Break out of your bubble.

POP!

From echo chambers to always hanging with the same crowd, doing the same things the same way means things will never change...

93.
Call.

Don't
text.

94.

Can you remember the sonnet from #25?

....

....

....

....

....

....

....

....

....

....

....

95.

Take your date to the supermarket.

After all, you have to
start somewhere...

(And you'll discover early on
whether you share the same tastes.)

96.

Cook up this simple recipe for two:

<u>Linguine alle Vongole</u>

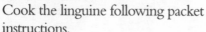

150g dried linguine
splash of olive oil
2 cloves garlic
pinch of dried red chilli flakes
1 bunch flat-leaf parsley
500g clams
125ml dry white wine
pinch of salt

Cook the linguine following packet instructions.

Meanwhile, heat the oil in a large pan, add the garlic and chilli and fry gently for 1 minute. Stir in the tomatoes, then add the clams and the wine and bring to the boil.

Cover the pan and cook for 3-4 mins, until the clams are open.

Season and serve.

97. Design a love emoji just for you and your crush to use.

98.

Arrange a rendezvous with a view, in the style of *Sleepless in Seattle*.

99.

Think of your favourite pop song and change the lyrics so they are about your sweetheart.

100.

Sometimes, the oldest truisms are the best:

Relax.
___

Be yourself.
___

Let the world come to you.